YOUR KNOWLEDGE HAS VALUE

Lee Hooper

Nonviolent Communication (NVC) in Education

Annotated Bibliography

GRIN Verlag

Bibliografische Information der Deutschen Nationalbibliothek:

Die Deutsche Bibliothek verzeichnet diese Publikation in der Deutschen National-
bibliografie; detaillierte bibliografische Daten sind im Internet über http://dnb.d-
nb.de/ abrufbar.

Imprint:

Copyright © 2013 GRIN Verlag GmbH
Druck und Bindung: Books on Demand GmbH, Norderstedt Germany
ISBN: 978-3-656-51243-1

This book at GRIN:

http://www.grin.com/en/e-book/262262/nonviolent-communication-nvc-in-education

GRIN - Your knowledge has value

Der GRIN Verlag publiziert seit 1998 wissenschaftliche Arbeiten von Studenten, Hochschullehrern und anderen Akademikern als eBook und gedrucktes Buch. Die Verlagswebsite www.grin.com ist die ideale Plattform zur Veröffentlichung von Hausarbeiten, Abschlussarbeiten, wissenschaftlichen Aufsätzen, Dissertationen und Fachbüchern.

Visit us on the internet:

http://www.grin.com/

http://www.facebook.com/grincom

http://www.twitter.com/grin_com

253.750 – Assignment 2

Annotated Bibliography: NVC in Education

Submitted on August 1st 2013

Introduction

Nonviolent communication (NVC) is an approach to create empathetic and honest connection amongst people using communicative techniques. NVC was first developed by Rosenberg (2003) in the 1960s. The principles of NVC are based on humanistic concepts from theorists such as Rogers, Maslow, and Fromm. NVC theory proposes that conflicts result from habitual communicative patterns whereby violent language based on emotions such as fear, guilt and anger, are used to try and meet one's need. Universal feelings and needs are a major key point of this theory. NVC recommends the use of a four step process to help bring clarity and awareness into communication. These steps are based on observations, feelings, needs, and requests. The first step involves differentiating between observations and evaluations, so specific behaviours and actions can be identified free of judgement. The second step is to become aware of what feelings are present. The third step is to find the underlying need behind the feeling. The last step involves requesting a concrete action that can help to meet that need. Rosenberg and Eisler (2003) argue that applying NVC principles into one's life can help us to see what is alive in ourselves, as well as in others.

This annotated bibliography will explore the influence that NVC has on education, particularly on the relationships between students and teachers. The significance of NVC in education is that it can provide a simple, yet effective way of developing connection between students and teachers at an increased rate (Hart & Kindle-Hodson, 2003). Furthermore, teachers are able to 'see' the needs behind the actions of the students, which can help them understand specific behaviours and act in accordance. Overall, there is a dearth of relevant literature to examine and support NVC ideology. However, the research that is out there is supportive of its efficiency and effectiveness. It is hoped that this paper will draw together some of the major works of NVC in relation to education and provide a systematic analysis on the relevant literature. Criteria for inclusion into this annotated bibliography surrounded material published within the last 12 years and a topic that either directly investigated NVC theory or NVC practice. The one exclusion is Cooper's (2009) article, which was included because of the lack of NVC studies in schools, and the articles relevance to NVC theory. Search engines used included Massey's *Discover*, with the key words, "("nonviolent communication" OR "non violent communication") AND (education* OR school*)", alongside the Centre for nonviolent communication's (cnvc.org) research section of their webpage.

YOUR TOPIC: NVC in Education

Reference:

Cooper, M. (2009). Counselling in UK secondary schools: a comprehensive review of audit and
evaluation data. *Counselling & Psychotherapy Research, 9*(3), 137-150.

FORM NO: 1   of   7

Keywords: Humanistic counselling, counselling in schools, meta-analysis, effectiveness

Relevance rating: 70%

Annotation:

Cooper's article on the effectiveness and efficiency of humanistic counselling in U.K
secondary schools provides both a comprehensive and critical analysis on the outcomes of this
theoretical approach. A meta review was conducted on a total of 30 studies involving approximately
10,000 clients. The author was able to identify quantitative statistics on who attended counselling
sessions and their reasons for doing so, alongside qualitative data, such as client and teacher
perspectives on the overall effectiveness of humanistic counselling within the schools. Cooper found
that humanistic school counselling was of benefit to around 80% of those who attended, a statistic
similar to cognitive behavioural therapy in U.S schools (Prout & Prout, 1998).

As Hanley, Sefi and Lennie (2011) note, whilst Cooper's review outlined many of the positive
aspects of counselling youth within schools, there were some limitations. These include not having
control groups so that intervention vs. non-intervention outcomes could be compared, and not
accounting for the fact that many of the students who completed the questionnaires mostly did so at
their final session. This meant that those who were disappointed and dropped out mid-way through,
may have not recorded their negative outcomes. Because of the lack of empirical data to support using
an NVC approach in an educational context and the large influence of humanistic thought on NVC
ideology, Cooper's study is significant as it helps to provide a foundational basis for using humanistic
approaches, such as NVC, within educational environments.

ANNOTATION FORM

YOUR TOPIC: NVC in Education

Reference:

Hart, S., & Göthlin, M. (2002). Lessons from the Skarpnäcks Free School. *Encounter, 15*(3), 38-42.

FORM NO:____2____of____7____

Keywords: _Communication in education, nonviolence, NVC, participatory education

Relevance rating: _90%

Annotation:

Lessons from the Skarpnäcks free school is a narrative written by Hart on Göthlin's experiences of setting up and running a predominately NVC based school in Sweden. During the four years of the school's existence, Göthlin points out that students have embraced the change from traditional school pedagogy to an NVC one, conflicts have significantly decreased, and standardised test show that students are performing at levels that either meet or exceed typical expectations. The main methods used by teachers include modelling NVC principles, replacing authoritarian demands with requests and participatory processes, as well as maintaining compassionate dialogue.

The strengths of this narrative lay in its critical appraisal of the methods used to teach NVC to the students and the observations noted by the teachers. For example, Göthlin identifies several problematic areas, such as finding time to create new teaching techniques and finding ways to incorporate the families of the students into learning NVC principles and participating in the learning process. In addition, Göthlin observed a correlation between age and habitual reactions. For example, younger students were more willing to adopt NVC ideology, such as making choices that met needs, instead of following commands. Those students who had already accustomed themselves to traditional school policy took more time to embrace this new way of thinking, with resistance lasting up to two years into the new schooling process. The weakness of this narrative is that the key elements that were being focused on; creating NVC dialogues, hearing the needs behind students' reactions, and establishing a community around the school, were not clearly identified from the start. Furthermore, a greater theoretical account for the problems faced at Skarpnäcks free school would have provided a more complex and comprehensive picture.

ANNOTATION FORM

YOUR TOPIC: NVC in Education

Reference:

Hart, S., & Kindle-Hodson, V. (2003). *The compassionate classroom: Relationship-based teaching and learning* (Chapter 5: Develop skills through activities and games, pp. 113-174). Encinitas, CA: PuddleDancer Press.

FORM NO: ___3___ of ___7___

Keywords: _NVC games and activities, teaching methods, education, compassionate classrooms_

Relevance rating: _90%_

Annotation:

This chapter looks to provide practical and concrete games and activities that can be applied in a classroom setting. The games and activities are centred on integrating the main tenets of NVC into workable systems that students can progress through in order to fully understand the concepts of NVC. They are categorised into observations, feelings, needs, listening, anger, daily communication, and a whole model approach. Overall, while Hart & Kindle-Hodson touch on philosophical, spiritual, and emotional matters, this book mainly deals with micro issues within the classroom, as its main intention is to help teaching professionals create compassionate and empathetic educational environments.

Many of the games illustrated by Hart and Kindle-Hodson seem simple in design and perhaps are catered towards students that are in primary school. Whether they would be able to hold the attention of high school students is questionable. However, if the principles behind them are adapted to suit a wider audience, they could be very promising. In addition, as Jeong-en (2004) argues, Hart and Kindle-Hodson neglect to account for the political landscape that students and teachers find themselves in, one that heavily influences and often predetermines actions and behaviours. Without addressing the institutional organisations involved in education simultaneously, the long term effectiveness of these games and activities can be called into question. However, despite this criticism, it is believed that the benefit in teaching NVC to school students through these types of games and activities is justified as short term outcomes of increased compassion and empathy will likely transgress into habitual usage, particularly if enough time is spent on them.

YOUR TOPIC: NVC in Education

Reference:

Jones, S. (2009). *Traditional Education or Partnership Education: Which Educational Approach Might Best Prepare Students for the Future?* (Unpublished master's thesis). San Diego University, San Diego: CA.

FORM NO: ___4___ of ___7___

Keywords: _NVC theory, educational strategies, partnership education, compassion and empathy_

Relevance rating: __80%__

Annotation:

In this thesis, Jones presents an alternative approach to teaching. Traditional hierarchical educational pedagogies are examined with an emphasis on power relations. This process is illustrated by dominant teaching practices that control the learning process and educational environment. Jones argues that educational strategies based on control and dominance are likely to stifle the learning process and create a climate which is not conducive to empathy and compassion. Instead, Jones states that utilising NVC based techniques, which rely on partnership, help to establish trust, compassion and empathy. The main purpose of this study was to offer empathy training, based on NVC principles to graduate teaching assistants (GTAs) in K-8 school. The results of this study demonstrated an increase in self-reported compassion, respect, empathy, and connection between GTAs and students, showing an overall positive outcome.

Like Hora and Miller (2011), Jones sees the value in creating partnership education as a way to positively influence and affect the learning process. The strength of this study is Jones' attention to providing theoretical explanations of the concepts used within the paper. Emphasis is placed on explaining the framework behind partnership education and why it is so valuable. One of the potential limitations of the study was that GTAs were only given one 45 minute session on empathy. Whilst Jones believed this to be adequate, perhaps longer and more frequent workshops would have yielded better results. Overall, Jones gives a comprehensive account of NVC concepts and partnership education theory.

YOUR TOPIC: NVC in Education

Reference:

Pedersen, A., & Rasmussen, C. (2008). Conflict and communication: learning a new language. *Race Equality Teaching, 26*(2), 44-48.

FORM NO: 5   of   7

Keywords: NVC, nonviolent communication, conflict resolution, education

Relevance rating: 90%

Annotation:

This paper looks to give a brief account on the inclusion of NVC into the Danish school system, at both the primary and secondary school level. The focus of this article is to introduce practical ways to implement NVC into the classroom setting, paying particular attention to conflict resolution. Examples are given to students demonstrating how conflicts are either resolved or escalated by the language we use. This is done through role-playing, storytelling, and providing visual aids. An emphasis on teacher role modelling is also apparent throughout this article.

Like Boal (1998), Pedersen and Rasmussen argue that participation in drama exercises can help students to understand conflict through acting it out. Similar to Finson & Pederson (2011), the importance of providing visual aid is also recognised in an education setting. Overall, Pedersen and Rasmussen make an argument that education should focus more on personal and social skills training, as opposed to what Mayo (2009) characterises as the dominant discourse of achieving academic competence. Unfortunately the authors only contribute anecdotal evidence on the success of implementing NVC within these schools. If empirical research had been done to support their findings then a much stronger argument would have been made.

ANNOTATION FORM

YOUR TOPIC: NVC in Education

Reference:

Rosenberg, M. (2003). *Nonviolent communication: A language of life*. Encinitas, CA: PuddleDancer
Press.

Keywords: _NVC, nonviolent communication, Marshall Rosenberg, giraffe language_

Relevance rating: _95%_

Annotation:

Rosenberg's book on NVC looks to provide a basic understanding of the main tenets of NVC
theory and practice, including the four components of NVC, communication that blocks compassion,
receiving empathetically, and expressing anger in a clean and constructive way. Examples are given
throughout the book on how to incorporate NVC theory into practice, typically at the end of each
chapter. Rosenberg illustrates NVC concepts through the use of *giraffe* language; a process whereby
an individual is conscious of their feelings and needs, so that empathetic listening and honest
expressing is a natural state. This is in opposition to *jackal* language, which is based on judgement and
often unconscious and reactive processes. Overall, Rosenberg's main intention in this book is to create
a grassroots movement amongst the public sphere, so that universal needs are more likely to be met.

As Veliyannoor (2010) points out, since this book is aimed at providing practical tools for
those interested in NVC, it often falls short on presenting a theoretical account for many of the basic
principles of the theory. Furthermore, many of the assumptions, such as universal needs, the idea that
all action represents an attempt to meet these needs, and premise that choice is internal, have not been
fully substantiated. However, in line with Kohn's (1999) account of intrinsic motivation leading to a
fulfilment of internal needs, and Tay and Diener's (2011) report on the commonality of needs and
subjective wellbeing across the world, evidence to support Rosenberg's conceptual theories is
available. One point that could be addressed in Rosenberg's future works is to avoid over
simplification of NVC's theoretical framework, and instead clarify in more detail its structural and
functional components.

YOUR TOPIC: NVC in Education

Reference:

Young, L. B. (2011). The expression of nonviolence in communication and its relation to physical and
    mental health: Development and validation of a coding system for measuring the expression of
    nonviolence in communication between intimate partners in conflict situations. *Dissertation
    Abstracts International, 72*(19b), 5585.

FORM NO: _____7_____ of _____7_____

Keywords: _NVC, coding system, nonviolence, communication_

Relevance rating: _75%_

Annotation:

    In this study, Young assesses the effectiveness of a coding system specifically designed for
NVC data analysis. Recruiting 247 intimate couples from university, Young's intention was to
measure the level of nonviolence during communication in a single scenario involving conflict,
alongside the validity of the various coding systems. Using a combination of several other coding
methods, such as a positive and negative affect schedule, nonviolent predisposition and an NVC
inventory, communication acts were coded into ten distinct patterns, such as intensity, intention and
tone. Young's results support the effectiveness of several aspects of this newly comprised NVC
coding system, as nonviolence could be detected and measured in what was said, alongside how it was
said.

    As Punch (2009) notes, using coding systems is an important part of research as it facilitates
analysis and increases the reliability of data. In order to be proven accurate, coding systems must be
tested and peer-reviewed. Since Young's research was a pilot study and is relatively new, it remains to
be verified. Whilst this study did not take place within an education setting, its relevance lays in the
fact that there is a large gap in NVC research. In helping to create and validate an NVC coding system
in this setting, it is hoped that further investigation and refinement will take place and that an NVC
coding system applicable to education may be developed some time in the near future.

Conclusion

Throughout this annotated bibliography relevant journal articles and books were critical analysed in order to assess the impact and influence of NVC on education. The theoretical background of NVC was empirically validated in Cooper's (2009) study on humanistic school counselling. Rosenberg's (2003) fundamental book outlined the core tenets of NVC ideology, whilst Hart and Kindle-Hodson (2003) provided concrete ways to implement NVC into schools. Pedersen and Rasmussen (2008) as well as Hart and Göthlin (2002) outlined their experiences as teachers in NVC schools, illustrating the strengths and limitations of this approach. Jones (2009) summarised on how partnership educational processes, such as NVC, were of much more value than traditionally based approaches. Finally, Young (2011) presented a coding tool that can contribute to future research in NVC.

Overall, the research used to compile this annotated bibliography demonstrated that empirical evidence does exist to support the application of NVC within an educational environment, particularly in relation to conflict resolution and increasing empathy and understanding in the classroom. On a personal note, I discovered that the current research validates what I have experienced in my own life when using NVC as a tool for connection; that it accelerates it. In retrospection, narrowing down the topic to a certain aspect of education, such as behaviour, conflict, or academic success, would have been interesting. However, due to limited research being done in this field, having a more general topic proved to be more viable. In conclusion, the research provided in this annotated bibliography illustrates the potential of NVC in facilitating connection, and meeting the needs of all those involved. It is hoped that further research will be undertaken in the future so that NVC can gain recognition and prominence in the field on education.

References

Boal, A. (1998). *Legislative theatre*. London, U.K: Routledge.

Cooper, M. (2009). Counselling in UK secondary schools: a comprehensive review of audit and evaluation data. *Counselling & Psychotherapy Research, 9*(3), 137-150.

Finson, K., & Pederson, J. (2011). What are visual data and what utility do they have in science education?. *Journal of Visual Literacy, 30*(1), 66-85.

Hanley, T., Sefi, A., & Lennie, C. (2011). Practice-based evidence in school-based counselling. *Counselling & Psychotherapy Research, 11*(4), 300-309.

Hart, S., & Göthlin, M. (2002). Lessons from the Skarpnäcks Free School. *Encounter, 15*(3), 38-42.

Hart, S., & Kindle-Hodson, V. (2003). *The compassionate classroom: Relationship-based teaching and learning*. Encinitas, CA: PuddleDancer Press.

Hora, M., & Miller, S. (2011). A guide to building education partnerships: Navigating diverse cultural contexts to turn challenge into promise. Sterling, VA: Stylus Publishing

Jeong-en, R. (2004). The Compassionate Classroom: Relationship Based Teaching and Learning (Book). *Encounter, 17*(2), 57-59.

Jones, S. (2009). *Traditional Education or Partnership Education: Which Educational Approach Might Best Prepare Students for the Future?* (Unpublished master's thesis). San Diego University, San Diego: CA.

Kohn, A. (1999). *Punished by rewards: The trouble with gold stars, incentive plans, A's, praise, and other bribes*. Boston, MA: Houghton Mifflin.

Mayo, P. (2009). The 'competence' discourse in education and the struggle for social agency and critical citizenship. *International Journal of Educational Policies, 3*(2), 5-16.

Pedersen, A., & Rasmussen, C. (2008). Conflict and communication: learning a new language. *Race Equality Teaching, 26*(2), 44-48.

Prout, S.M., & Prout, H.T. (1998). A meta-analysis of school-based studies of counseling and psychotherapy: An update. *Journal of School Psychology, 36*(2), 121-136.

Punch, K. (2009). *Introduction to research methods in education*. Los Angeles, CA: Sage Publications.

Rosenberg, M. (2003). *Nonviolent communication: A language of life*. Encinitas, CA: PuddleDancer Press.

Rosenberg, M., & Eisler, R. (2003). *Life-enriching education: Nonviolent communication helps schools improve performance, reduce conflict, and enhance relationships*. Encinitas, CA: PuddleDancer Press.

Tay, L., & Diener, E. (2011). Needs and subjective well-being around the world. *Journal of Personality and Social Psychology, 101*(2), 354-365.

Young, L. B. (2012). The expression of nonviolence in communication and its relation to physical and mental health: Development and validation of a coding system for measuring the expression of nonviolence in communication between intimate partners in conflict situations. *Dissertation Abstracts International, 72*(19b), 5585.

Veliyannoor, P. (2010). Book review. *Sanyasa Journal of Consecrated Life, 5*(1), 99-101.